HOW TO GRADUATE

FROM PEOPLE COLLEGE

SERIES 1: THE

BEGINNING

APOSTLE JANICE GRIER

Contents

Foreword

Have you ever thought about failing in school, sports, relationships or any other activity that requires interacting with others? Daily we interact with other people in ways that help to form our interpersonal skills. Our people skills can be affected in positive as well as negative ways simply by the foundation of our past.

We have all failed "people courses" at some point in life, but what if we had a tool to help us reshape the way in which we interact with others? What if we had a step by step guide to help us mend broken fences, broken hearts and move past the generational issues of our past and walk into the newness of our destiny? If you have been on a relentless cycle of people pleasing, people failures and people stumbling blocks, today is the day that you can change the stinking people skills for a fresh new course that will revolutionize your people skills.

How to Graduate from People College is your tool to help you walk into the fullness of interacting with the people around you. It will also help you as you forge new relationships that are healthy and prosperous.

I believe Apostle Janice Grier has unlocked key

Foreword

elements that will help you close the doors to negative and unhealthy relationships. This book is just the beginning of helping you unlock the people skills that will change your life.

Dr. Jacquie Hadnot
Author and Empowerment Speaker

Foreword

Dedication

I want to thank My Lord and savior Jesus Christ for this awesome revelation that will cause others to be motivated to go through the basic courses of life and be able to pass with Honors!

To my faithful, loving husband Co-Pastor Patrick Grier who has been the wind beneath my wings through ministry and life moments.

To my precious children and their spouses Falisha (Derrick) Smith, Jonathan (Keshonnon) Spence and my awesome grandchildren Benji and Psalms.

In addition, to the best church for me, New and

Dedication

Living Way International Deliverance Ministries in Tucker, Georgia. Thank you for your much love and support.

To my dear friend Dr Jackie Hadnot for pushing me to birth this great book for God's glory.

Thank you for believing in me my beautiful Aunt Hazel Mitchell of Covington, Georgia.

Introduction

This book provides information on how we must be able to recognize and deal with the different emotions and frustrations that we carry from birth to adulthood, which causes us to become "people pleasers." It includes an insight on the different courses that we must learn from, and pass to be able to graduate from the college called "People College."

As you take the journey throughout this book, I pray that your experience will be so satisfying that you will find yourself no longer a victim to

Introduction

people's opinions, but a victor in confidence and self-worth, by knowing that God made you unique according to His pattern. Emotions such as rejection, low self-esteem, insecurity, fear, and inferiority, will make us slaves to the will of people.

The purpose of this book is to enhance your prayer life, and to inspire you to develop a passionate relationship with God. The purpose is also to strengthen you in your walk with the Lord and for you to experience a great manifestation of divine destiny in your life.

HOW TO GRADUATE

FROM PEOPLE COLLEGE

SERIES 1: THE

BEGINNING

APOSTLE JANICE GRIER

Chapter 1

HOW TO GRADUATE FROM PEOPLE COLLEGE

LET'S GET STARTED

Many people cannot go forth in life because of what someone thinks of them, so they live their lives through others. I remember when I was a little girl in the 4th grade, I felt like I had to be a class clown or give gifts for people to approve of me. These types of actions continued throughout high school. I always felt like I had to give something or do something for people to like me.

What I did not realize is that I was born in the spirit of rejection which caused me to find myself over-compensating to get people to like me. Why? Because my mother conceived me at 13 years old. She was just a baby herself so my grandmother raised me until I was 8 years old. At age eight, my

> *Many people cannot go forth in life because of what someone thinks of them, so they live their lives through others.*

mother married and began having babies one right after the other. She decided to come and take me from my grandmother's house to help take care of the babies she conceived with my stepfather. I knew my mother loved me in her own way, but I still did not like the fact that she

16

came and took me from my grandmother's house all because she needed a babysitter. I believed I had to do extra things to make my mother love me. I never experienced a sense of belonging to the family because I was always trying to prove myself to my mother and stepfather.

When I started school, I continued to try to please others. In life, you must make up your mind that YOU CAN'T PLEASE EVERYBODY ALL THE TIME! You have to pass the courses entitled *Rejection* and *Low self-esteem*. If you don't pass these classes, your next class will be *Addiction Approval.*

HOW TO GRADUATE FROM PEOPLE COLLEGE
SERIES 1: THE BEGINNING

Chapter 2

THE LIFE COURSE OF REJECTION

We are born with certain generational traits from our mother and father that we must contend with from birth throughout adulthood. Psalm 51:5 says, *"Behold, I was shapen in iniquity; and in sin did my mother conceive me."* Nevertheless, we must know how to recognize and live through generational traits such as low self-esteem, poverty, rejection, insecurity and inferiority.

Please let us not forget about the spirit of fear that comes upon us and immobilizes us so that we cannot move forward in life, all because of what someone said or did to us.

Paul gave us a course of action in Philippians 3:13-14 that can help us get started with our undergraduate class

> *We must know how to recognize and live through generational traits such as low self-esteem, poverty, rejection, insecurity and inferiority.*

of overcoming people. It states: *"Brethren, I count not myself to have apprehended: but this one thing I do, forgetting those things which are behind, and reaching forth unto those things which are before, I press toward the mark for the prize of the high calling of God in Christ Jesus."* This scripture is like a drink of fresh water on a thirsty mind suffering from confusion and instability of direction.

Rejection is a trait we all suffer from in one way or another. Roget's II New Thesaurus defines rejection as a negative response, a refusal, denial, a turn down of someone or something.

Rejection causes you to become afflicted with other unwanted soul ties, such as depression, oppression, self-denial, pride, and lack of worth in one's self. The Bible states in Psalms 34:19, *"Many are the afflictions of the righteous: but the Lord delivereth him out of them all."*

HOW TO GRADUATE FROM PEOPLE COLLEGE
SERIES 1: THE BEGINNING

Chapter 3

ME, MYSELF, AND I

In this college called *"Overcoming People"* you must make up your mind that you are being prepared to work on the areas of your life called: Me, Myself and I.

You cannot excel in this life's college until you know what you are dealing with from birth. Do we know ourselves well enough to live free from the clutter of people pleasing emotions? Good question! In order to answer it we must deal with the three worst enemies of our life - me, myself, and I. We cannot overlook these three comrades that are with us daily! Because at the end of the day when we are finished with all the things in life that we think defines us as successful human beings, we still have to identify and

> *You cannot excel in this life's college until you know what you are dealing with from birth.*

overcome these three companions in our daily life and only God can help us to know ourselves. He knows our ways. Psalms 139-3 says, *"Thou compassest my path and my lying down, and art acquainted with all my Ways."*

Chapter 4

DON'T STAY THAT WAY

We came out of the womb sinful, but we do not have to stay that way! We are supposed to understand as we get older why we were created and formed in our mother's womb. Jeremiah 1:5 (AMP) states, *"Before I formed you in the womb I knew [and] approved of you [as my chosen instrument], and before you were born I separated and set you apart, consecrating you; [and] I appointed you as a prophet to the nations."* This scripture lets us know that change is already in our future as we grow.

To pass the test of rejection and addiction approval, you must study the lesson plans of long**-suffering, and forgiveness...**

<u>Definition of Longsuffering</u> - The capacity of enduring hardship or inconvenience without complaint: forbearance, patience, and tolerance. (Roget's II the New Thesaurus).

> *We must learn the word forgiveness daily in order to go forth with steady speed in life.*

Roget's **definition of Forgiveness:** The act or an instance of forgiving, absolution, amnesty, excused, pardon, remission.

II Timothy 2-3 tells us, *"Thou therefore endure hardness, as a good soldier of Jesus Christ."*

We will endure some things in this life that will seem to be hard on our life, but through these hardships comes the victory! Because the tests, the tribulations, and persecutions in our lives are the professors that push us to our ultimate goal of finishing with Honors. We must be able to tolerate and learn what is the very essence of patience in our lives because it is important for us to finish strong.

We must learn the word forgiveness daily in order to go forth with steady speed in life. Jesus taught us a lesson in His walk with men. The lesson was always forgiveness. Jesus taught the disciples in Matthew 6-12, the model prayer; *"And forgive us our debts, as we forgive our debtors"*… also the 14th verse states, *"For if we forgive men their trespasses, your heavenly Father will also forgive you."* To move forth in

People College we have to master the course of forgiveness. Unless we forgive others for what they have done to us, we will not be able to have a clear future. **Your past must be fired so your future can be hired!**

Chapter 5

FORGIVE, SO YOU CAN BEGIN TO LIVE: JUDGE NOT, THAT YE BE NOT JUDGED

"Judge not, that ye be not judged. For with what judgment ye judge, ye shall be judged; and with what measure ye mete, it shall be measured to you again."

Matthew 7:1-2

We have to be careful how we sit in judgment of others while we are moving through the portal of life, because we must first get ourselves together before we can help someone else. Matthew 7:5 clearly states to our benefit, *"Thou hypocrite, first cast out the beam out of thine own eye; and then*

> *We have to be careful how we sit in judgment of others while we are moving through the portal of life.*

shalt thou see clearly to cast out the mote out of thy brother's eye." As we study and continue to learn how to submit our emotions and will to God's plan for our lives, we can help others to pass the course. We have to work on ourselves daily by denouncing the soul ties of our past. To denounce something means to condemn or to feel a strong disapproval of something. I discovered that I had to condemn the generational traits in my family line before I could go forth. I noticed that all the girls in my family became pregnant at the age of 13 including my Mother. As I grew up, I learned it was a generational curse, so I decided to use the tool of denunciation and remove the roadblock that would prevent me from finishing high school.

I received Christ in my life at the age of 14 and developed a prayer life, which brought me into a close relationship with God. As I surrendered to His will in my life I denounced all generational curses, forefather curses, and ancestry soul-ties that are carried through the bloodline. I condemned these things daily as I was growing up and attending school. While denouncing I broke the curse and passed the test I graduated high school with honors and attended college.

But, before I could get to this point in my life I had to condemn and strongly disapprove of the generational roadblocks.

It is up you to stop the generational cycle of failure.

SOUL TIE RELEASE PRAYER

Father, in Jesus Name I come before you asking your forgiveness from the soul ties of my past and generational curses. Father, release me from the ungodly emotions that have formed a soul tie in my soul. I forgive the persons that were in my past that hurt me, abused me and misused me. Therefore, I denounce all ungodly sexual and emotional relationships right now. Lord Your Word says in Psalms 103-12, *I confess my sins unto the Lord, He removes them from me as far as the east is from the west in Jesus name.* Amen.

This prayer must be read three times a day until it becomes a part of your daily routine.

HOW TO GRADUATE FROM PEOPLE COLLEGE
SERIES 1: THE BEGINNING

Chapter 6

LOW SELF ESTEEM

This course deals with your confidence in yourself. People with low self esteem never ever live life to the fullest. They maintain a distance from other people and deny themselves love and care from family and friends.

You must change your mind set about who you are in life and Christ. Psalms 139: 13-14, *"For thou hast possessed my reins: thou hast covered me in my mother's womb. I will praise thee; for I am fearfully and wonderfully made marvelous are thy works; and that my soul knoweth right well."*

This scripture reminds me daily that God does not make Junk! I was carefully made according to His divine pattern. I must be what God has designed me to be and not someone else. When we embrace the above concept in our spirit, soul, and mind then we can successfully complete the course of LOW SELF ESTEEM.

> *God does not make **Junk!***

Chapter 7

FEAR

To graduate from People College we must pass the course of fear. An anonymous writer wrote an acronym for fear. F.E.A.R is:

F-False

E- Evidence

A-Appearing

R- Real

However, to pass the course you must study. 2 Timothy 1:7 (KJV) states: *"For God hath not given us the spirit of fear; but of power, and of love, and of a sound mind."* The amplified version 2 Timothy 1:7 states, *"For God did not give us a spirit of timidity (of cowardice, of craven and cringing and fawning fear), but [He has given us a spirit] of power and of love and of calm and well-balanced mind and discipline and self-control."* These are words to remember in order to help you pass the course.

Fear is a course that everyone deals with, but passing with honors is sometimes difficult. First, you have to detect what is fearful about your life!

I can remember when I was so afraid of what certain people thought about me, that I would do things to get approval from them in some way or another, because I carried the fear of being Rejected or overlooked. But I found out that no matter what you do for people they will never be completely satisfied with who you are. Therefore, you have to be yourself and stay true to God.

Most people are afraid of the unknown and that is why they will not take risks, or believe in what they cannot see. I found myself getting delivered from fear when I read and understood II Timothy 1-7. The following three words power, love, and sound mind are the keys. Power (dunamis, absolute), Love (hides, forgives, covers), and Sound Mind (peace, wholeness, completeness, joy). These keys unlock spiritual weapons that I used to walk in complete victory from the very obstacle of fear.

I am writing this first series of 'HOW TO

GRADUATE FROM PEOPLE COLLEGE, because I want you know that you can live life in abundance without being worried about who will like you today.

My personal testimony is one of rejection, low self-esteem, self–denial, poverty, addiction approvals and fear. Nevertheless, I am here by the grace and mercy

> *You have to be yourself, and stay true to God.*

of God. When I accepted Jesus Christ as my Lord and Savior, people said I would not stay saved. Not only did I get saved, I received the gift of the precious Holy Ghost (the Keeper). I have been submitted to God for over 49 years and loving every minute of this journey.

I have been young and single in school and through college, single and saved, married and saved and I still put God first in my life at all times. To pass in these areas of our life we must surrender totally to God's will. James 4-7: *"Submit yourselves (flesh) therefore to God. Resist (spiritual warfare) the devil, and he will flee from you."* (Let go, and let God).

People said I wouldn't make it after I established the ministry of New and Living Way International Deliverance Ministries, **but look at God**! We are still growing in quantity and quality. I must encourage you to look to the hills from whence comes your help; your help comes from the Lord and not people. *"If it had not been the LORD who was on our side, now may Israel* *say; If it had not been the LORD who was on our side, when men rose up against us"* (Psalm. 124: 1-2). I took the courses, did the homework, passed the classes and graduated from People College. It was all through His amazing Grace and you can, also. I stand today as a graduate of People College through His amazing Grace.

Knowing life is not easy, but move forth with determination.

Chapter 8

Conclusion: How to Graduate

To graduate from People College, you must carry a 3.0 – the biblical number of the trinity (Father, Son and the Holy Ghost).

I must emphasize the word *relationship* because this is our triune God. We must maintain an intimate relationship with our Father to succeed and complete the course that is before us. Three means complete. While going through life we must be complete in our walk and in our understanding of God's plan for us. We can complete assignments when we have a good relationship with God.

I know that if I did not have a relationship with the triune God, I would not have made it through my childhood, teen years, or adulthood. My classes started at age 14 when God came into my life and gave me

> *While going through life we must be complete in our walk and in our understanding of Gods plan for us.*

a reason to live, and the ability to overcome the way people looked at me. Being saved at an early age was not easy, but I began to use the tools that God gave me to pass my test of life. These tools are reading his word (Bible), developing an effective prayer life, praise, worship, and consistently keeping me, Janice, before Him in personal prayer. We must remember the Triune is relational, not a religious idea.

HOW TO GRADUATE FROM PEOPLE COLLEGE
SERIES 1: THE BEGINNING

SCRIPTURES TO HELP PASS THE EXAMS OF LIFE

PSALMS 23:1-2

PROVERBS 3:26

I JOHN 5:4

HEBREWS 13:6

ISAIAH 41:10

II TIMOTHY 1:7

ROMANS 10:7

DEUTERONOMY 28:12-13

HOW TO GRADUATE FROM PEOPLE COLLEGE
SERIES 1: THE BEGINNING

NOTES

_____

_____

_____

_____

_____

_____

_____

_____

_____

HOW TO GRADUATE FROM PEOPLE COLLEGE
SERIES 1: THE BEGINNING

_____

_____

_____

_____

_____

_____

_____

_____

_____

_____

_____

_____

HOW TO GRADUATE FROM PEOPLE COLLEGE
SERIES 1: THE BEGINNING

_____

_____

_____

_____

_____

_____

_____

_____

_____

_____

_____

_____

_____

_____

_____

_____

_____

_____

_____

_____

_____

_____

ABOUT

THE AUTHOR

HOW TO GRADUATE FROM PEOPLE COLLEGE
SERIES 1: THE BEGINNING

About the Author

Apostle Janice D. Grier received Christ into her life at the age of 14. She graduated from Newton County High School with honors, attended Georgia State College, and graduated in 1975. She continued to pursue her education at Dayspring Theological Seminary located in Panama City, Florida where she graduated in 2002.

Under the unction of the Holy Spirit, The Fellowship Church of Praise of Atlanta, GA was birthed on January 1, 2007. In 2009, under the divine guidance of God, Apostle Janice Grier founded The New and Living Way International Deliverance Ministries, in Tucker, GA. Her husband, Co-Pastor Elder Patrick H. Grier, is a prayer warrior and supports the vision and work of the ministry. He stands by her side and boldly proclaims the Gospel.

Apostle Janice Grier is an anointed woman of God and has been chosen by God to walk in the fivefold ministry. She moves in the area of healing and deliverance. Many people have been healed from terminal diseases in various areas of their lives.

Apostle Grier is spiritually motivated to work in the Kingdom. In 2007, she formed the Reach Beyond the Break Outreach Ministries - a community outreach program, which assists with food, clothing, housing and utility assistance in the Tucker, GA area. In addition, she is the founder of a prayer ministry called SWAT (Spiritual Warfare Action Team) formed in 2009. The prayer ministry teaches the concept of praying effectively. In 2013, she established the Fellowship of churches, Inc. with nine churches in the Fellowship.

In May 2011, Apostle Janice Grier made her presence known on the airwaves on Channel 57 and Comcast Channel 2. The dynamic teachings of the Apostle aired every Saturday morning on the 6 a.m. broadcast. With the favor of God on her life she continues on WATC 57, now broadcasting every Monday night at 6 p.m. Apostle Janice Grier founded J. Grier Christian Academy, which is licensed and incorporated by the State of Georgia.

Apostle Janice Grier formed Apostle Janice Grier Ministries in 2013 which is committed to serving

God and the community. It is an international ministry that desires to share the love of God and the importance of deliverance not only with the community but also with every nation.

Apostle Janice Grier stands firmly and walks boldly as a Kingdom Dominionaire! As God continues to speak through Apostle Grier, she continues to move expeditiously; by taking quantum leaps and bounds through faith. Her goal is to bring God's people into the maturity of Christ that they may walk in the New and Living Way.

HOW TO GRADUATE FROM PEOPLE COLLEGE
SERIES 1: THE BEGINNING

CONTACT APOSTLE JANICE GRIER

New and Living Way International
Deliverance Ministries
4018 Lawrenceville Highway
Tucker GA 30084
www.nlwintl.com
(770) 491-7200

For additional copies visit

www.amazon.com

HOW TO GRADUATE FROM PEOPLE COLLEGE
SERIES 1: THE BEGINNING